# MATERIALS THAT MATTER

# WOOD

## Neil Morris

W

FRANKLIN WATTS

LONDON • SYDNEY

An Appleseed Editions book

First published in 2010 by Franklin Watts
338 Euston Road, London NW1 3BH

Franklin Watts Australia
Hachette Children's Books
Level 17/207 Kent St, Sydney, NSW 2000

© 2010 Appleseed Editions

Created by Appleseed Editions Ltd,
Well House, Friars Hill, Guestling,
East Sussex TN35 4ET

Designed by Helen James
Edited by Mary-Jane Wilkins
Artwork by Graham Rosewarne
Picture research by Su Alexander

ISBN 978 1 4451 0025 8

Dewey Classification: 620.1'2

A CIP catalogue for this book is available from the British Library.

Photograph acknowledgements
page 4 Henry Westheim Photography/Alamy; 6 North Wind Picture Archives/Alamy;
7 Travelpixs/Alamy; 8 Bibliotheque de l'Arsenal Paris/Kharbine-Tapabor/Coll.Jean
Vigne/The Art Archive; 9 David Kilpatrick/Alamy; 10 Chris Luneski/Alamy; 11 & 12
Gunter Marx/Alamy; 14 Neil McAllister/Alamy; 15 Nordicphotos/Alamy; 16 H Mark
Weidman Photography/Alamy; 17 J Baylor Robots/NGS Image Collection/The Art
Archive; 18 James Hawkins/Alamy; 19 John James/Alamy; 20 Susan Yates/Alamy;
22 Tibor Bognar/Alamy; 23 Jeff Morgan Industry And Work/Alamy; 25 Photoshot
Holdings Ltd/Alamy; 26 Julio Etchart/Alamy; 27 Robert Harding Picture Library/Alamy;
28 Andrew N Gagg/Alamy; 29 Dennis Kunkel Microscopy Inc./Phototake/Alamy
Front cover Christine Osborne Pictures/Alamy

Printed in China

Franklin Watts is a division of Hachette Children's Books,
an Hachette UK company.
www.hachette.co.uk

# Contents

# What is wood?

You can probably think of lots of things that are made of wood. Your desk or table may be wooden. The pencil you write with may be made of wood, too. There are many different kinds of wood; some are very heavy while others are quite light. But they all come from the same source – trees.

*Wood comes in many shades of colour. It also has different grain (see page 15). You can see grain lines at the ends of these boards.*

## Part of a tree

Wood makes up the trunk and branches of trees. It is the main substance in all woody plants. Scientists call it plant tissue, or **xylem** (from the Greek word for wood). Trees use this tissue to carry water and minerals up from their roots.

When the liquid reaches a tree's leaves, they combine it with sunlight and **carbon dioxide** gas from the air. This process, called **photosynthesis**, helps plants to make their own sugary food (called sap). Liquid travels through the tiny cells that make up wood.

## USING WOOD AGAIN

Wood from buildings or furniture can be recycled when the original item is no longer needed (see pages 26-27 on recycling). The wood can be reused as it is, or it can be sawn up or ground down into wood chips.

Recycling helps the environment in many ways. If we recycle wood, we need to cut down fewer trees. We also use less energy than when we fell, saw and prepare new timber. This reduces **pollution** and the amount of waste we dump in landfill sites.

These cells are shaped like narrow, hollow tubes. There may be as many as 500 billion cells in one cubic metre of wood. The cells can also store sap for future use.

## Tiny fibres

The walls of wood cells are made mainly of a soft substance called **cellulose**. This word comes from the French *cellule*, meaning small cell. The tiny, threadlike fibres that make up cellulose are only a tenth of a millimetre wide and just over one millimetre long.

Cellulose makes up about half of the weight of wood. Another natural substance, called **lignin**, binds the tiny fibres together.

## Inside a tree trunk

When a tree is cut down, we can see two kinds of wood inside the trunk. Near the centre is a darker, drier section of **heartwood**. This is older wood that is dead but still helps to support the tree. The living cells of lighter, softer **sapwood** surround the heartwood. A layer of bark covers the outside of the trunk.

*Trees make a new layer of wood every year. The layers form growth rings, which tell us how old a tree was when it was felled. How old was this tree?*

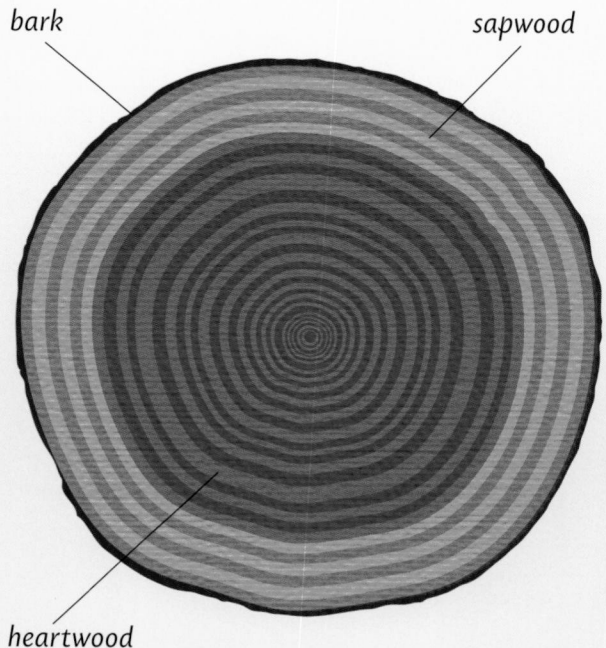

bark

sapwood

heartwood

# Fire, shelter and ships

There have been trees on Earth for hundreds of millions of years. The earliest human probably used fallen branches to dig for roots and other food, and to knock down fruits and nuts. Their descendants made tools and built shelters from wood, and also used it for making fire.

## The discovery of fire

Historians believe that humans first used wood to make controlled fires more than 500,000 years ago. **Prehistoric** humans may have seen lightning strike trees and set fire to them. This gave them the idea of lighting wood by making sparks. They made the sparks by rubbing sticks together or striking pieces of **flint**. Fire made a huge difference to people's lives. They used it to cook meat, which was then much easier and safer to eat. Fire provided warmth and light in caves and other shelters, as well as frightening away wild animals. The heat from fire was also useful for hardening stone and wooden tools.

*This nineteenth-century picture shows prehistoric humans making a fire.*

## Homes and hunting

Around 400,000 years ago, humans in Europe were using wood in new ways. At the site of Terra Amata in southern France, prehistoric people built oval-shaped wooden huts. They used strong branches to make these shelters. At around the same time, hunters at Schöningen in Germany were using sharp stone tools to cut two-metre long spears from spruce trees. The spears had sharp points and hunters threw them like javelins to kill wild animals.

## Early ships

The earliest boats were dugout canoes, which people hollowed out from tree trunks. The ancient Egyptians built boats from planks of wood nearly 5000 years ago. They found that the strongest planks came from the **cedar** trees which grew

*This boat was found beside the Great Pyramid at Giza in Egypt. The boat is at least 4500 years old and was rebuilt from 1200 pieces of cedar wood.*

in Lebanon. The ancient Greeks and Romans built larger wooden ships, both war **galleys** and merchant vessels. An ordinary Roman trading ship could carry hundreds of tonnes of grain from Egypt.

## Wooden tools

The first farmers used digging sticks and other wooden tools to help them plant crops. The wooden **plough** was invented about 8000 years ago and used to turn over the soil before farmers planted seeds. Later, iron was added to the plough's blade, to make it stronger.

### ROMAN PLANTING

Today we call wood a renewable resource, because new trees can be planted to replace those we chop down. The ancient Romans also planted trees, and brought seedlings to the Italian peninsula from all around their empire, including Lebanon. They planted groves of trees which gave them a constant supply of wood.

# Looking after forests

**Wood is a valuable material because it has so many uses. In prehistoric times there were plenty of trees in most parts of the world. But when people started farming, they made great gaps in the forests. They did this by harvesting wood and cutting down trees to make room for their crops, houses and animals.**

As settlements and villages grew into towns and cities, people chopped down more trees, and forests grew smaller. People living in towns needed wood for houses and furniture. Looking after the source of wood – trees – became important everywhere.

## Oaks for shipbuilding

During the Middle Ages in Europe, countries were using more and more wood to build ships. Britain, France, Portugal and Spain all built large navies. Their fleets of ships were for both trade and war. In England, King Henry VII (reigned 1485-1509) founded a dockyard at Portsmouth, where woodworkers built large cargo vessels. His son Henry VIII (reigned 1509-47) opened another dock on the River Thames, which built warships. Shipbuilders needed more than 2000 large oak trees

*A fifteenth-century French painting showing carpenters at work. The artist imagined that this was how Noah's ark was built.*

to make one of these ships. At this time, adventurous sailors were setting off around the world on voyages of discovery. They all travelled in wooden ships.

## Heating and cooking

Many people lived in timber-framed houses during the Middle Ages. In winter they burned huge amounts of wood to heat their homes and cook meals. By the seventeenth century, they were also burning large quantities of **charcoal**.

People made charcoal by heating wood in an enclosed space without air. This might be an oven or a pile of wood covered with **turf** or soil. Charcoal burned slowly and gave off great heat. During the eighteenth century, miners dug up great quantities of coal, but it was smoky and sooty when it burned. They wanted to go on burning wood or charcoal, but this meant cutting down more trees.

## Forest law

The process of cutting down trees and destroying forests is called **deforestation**. A document dating back to 1538 mentions deforesting and shows that even in those days people were aware of the problem.

### RENEWING A VALUABLE RESOURCE

Today, environmentalists stress the importance of renewable resources. By this they mean materials and sources of energy that do not run out when they are used, such as geothermal, solar, water and wind power. They also mean wood, which is used, but can be replaced by planting new trees. Good forest management makes this possible.

Kings and noblemen owned many forests, which they used for harvesting wood and hunting animals (for food and sport). Laws protecting forests were especially strong in France and Germany, where schools of forestry sprang up during the nineteenth century. Foresters realized that they had to manage woodland, and they planted new trees to replace those they cut down.

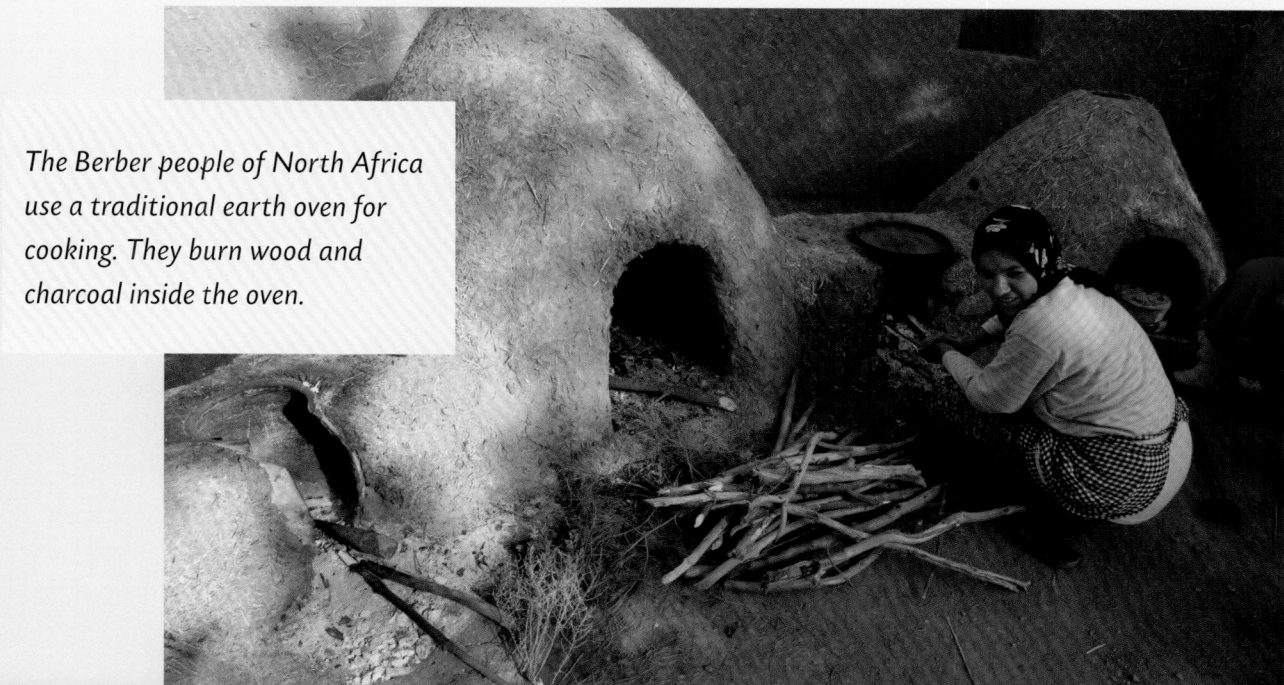

*The Berber people of North Africa use a traditional earth oven for cooking. They burn wood and charcoal inside the oven.*

# Felling trees for logs

**The job of felling trees and turning them into logs of wood is called logging. Loggers trim the felled trees to remove twigs and leaves, and transport the logs to a sawmill. There saws cut the logs into planks or boards (see pages 12-13). Foresters have to choose very carefully where they allow logging companies to fell trees.**

Today, most planted forests contain mainly **softwood** trees, and they are often made up of just one kind of tree. Older forests may have many different kinds of **hardwood** trees, which usually take longer to grow.

## Clearing or selecting

When loggers clear an area of forest, they chop down all the trees, but leave some branches and small pieces of wood from the felling to enrich the soil for new seedlings. Foresters then replant the area. Alternatively, loggers may select and cut down a number of older trees and leave the younger trees for future years.

## Chopping and sawing

Years ago, woodcutters chopped down trees with axes. Today, lumberjacks mostly use motor-driven chain saws to cut through the thick trunks. The saw's chain has a sharp cutting tooth on each link, and the chain moves around very fast. The tree feller cuts a wedge-shaped notch, or undercut, on the side of the trunk, facing the direction in which he wants the tree to fall. Cutting this notch takes some skill and it makes sure that a felled tree causes as little damage as possible to other trees and the workers.

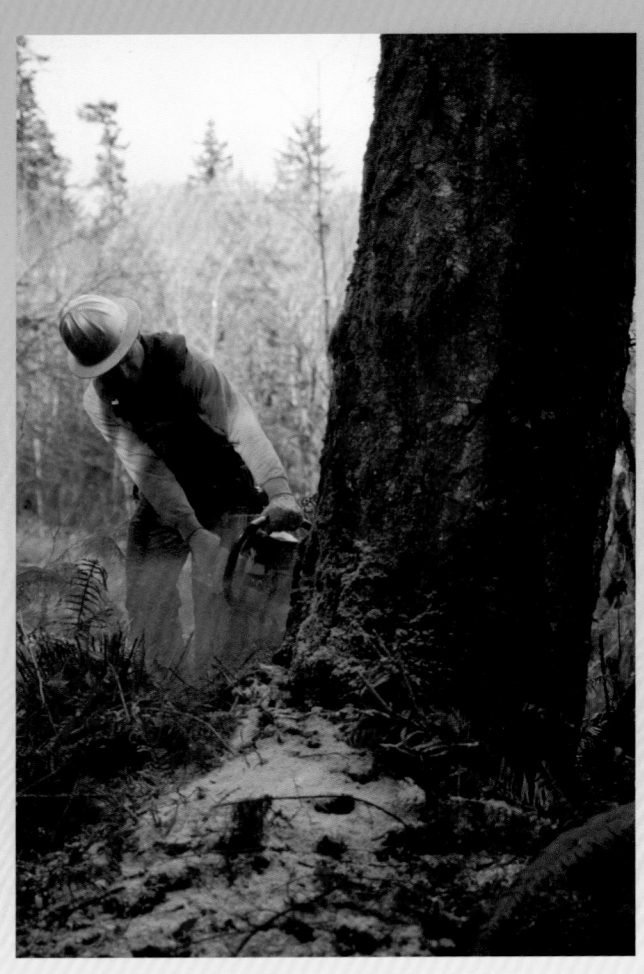

*A logger uses his chain saw to fell a tree in Oregon, USA.*

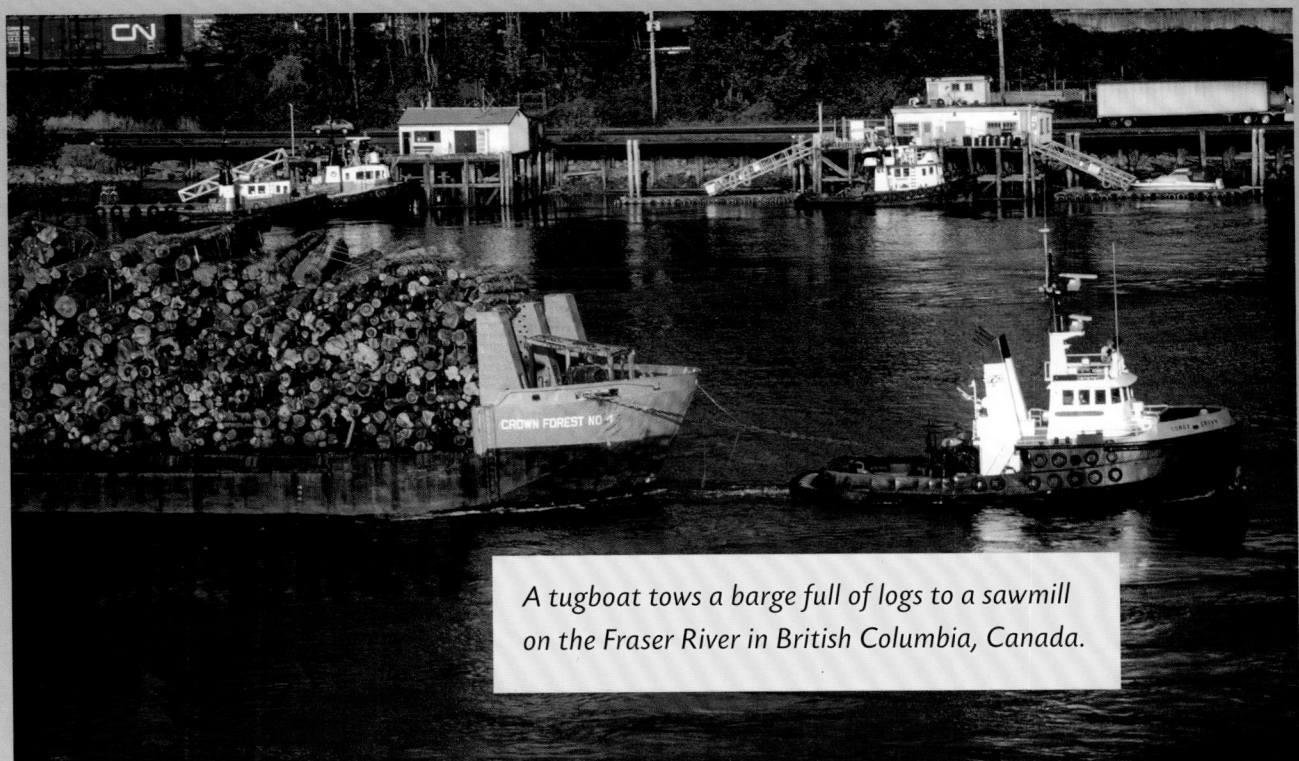

*A tugboat tows a barge full of logs to a sawmill on the Fraser River in British Columbia, Canada.*

## Dragging and driving

Loggers may cut the trees into smaller lengths before they take them away.

This depends on the size of the trees, what kind of wood they produce, and what the wood will be used for. Loggers use cranes or other machines to drag the logs to a clearing, where they are loaded on to lorries or railway wagons. These take the logs to the nearest sawmill.

## HARDWOOD AND SOFTWOOD

Hardwood comes from broad-leaved trees, such as birch, elm or oak. Most hardwood trees are **deciduous**, which means they drop their leaves in autumn. Softwood comes from needle-leaved trees, such as cedar, fir or pine. Most softwood trees are **evergreen**, which means they keep their leaves all year round. Most softwood trees are also conifers, which means they grow their seeds in cones.

## World's top loggers

Six countries together produce nearly half the world's wood.

| Country | Million cubic metres |
| --- | --- |
| USA | 444 |
| India | 330 |
| China | 294 |
| Brazil | 245 |
| Russia | 207 |
| Canada | 196 |

# At the sawmill

The sawmill has large power-driven saws, which cut logs into boards and planks. Centuries ago, water power drove the saws. Today, most are driven by electricity or natural gas, and many provide their own power by burning waste wood. The sawmills keep down the amount of waste wood they create by using computers to work out the best way to cut the wood.

## Cutting and sawing

First mechanical cutters take the bark off the logs. A conveyor chain then carries the logs to the head saw, which cuts the log into a chosen pattern. Computers work out the best pattern and guide the saw as the log moves back and forth. Next, band saws and circular saws cut the blocks of wood into different-sized planks and boards. Some of these are sliced again into thinner boards. These go through more saws, called edgers and thinners, which cut them into standard lengths and widths.

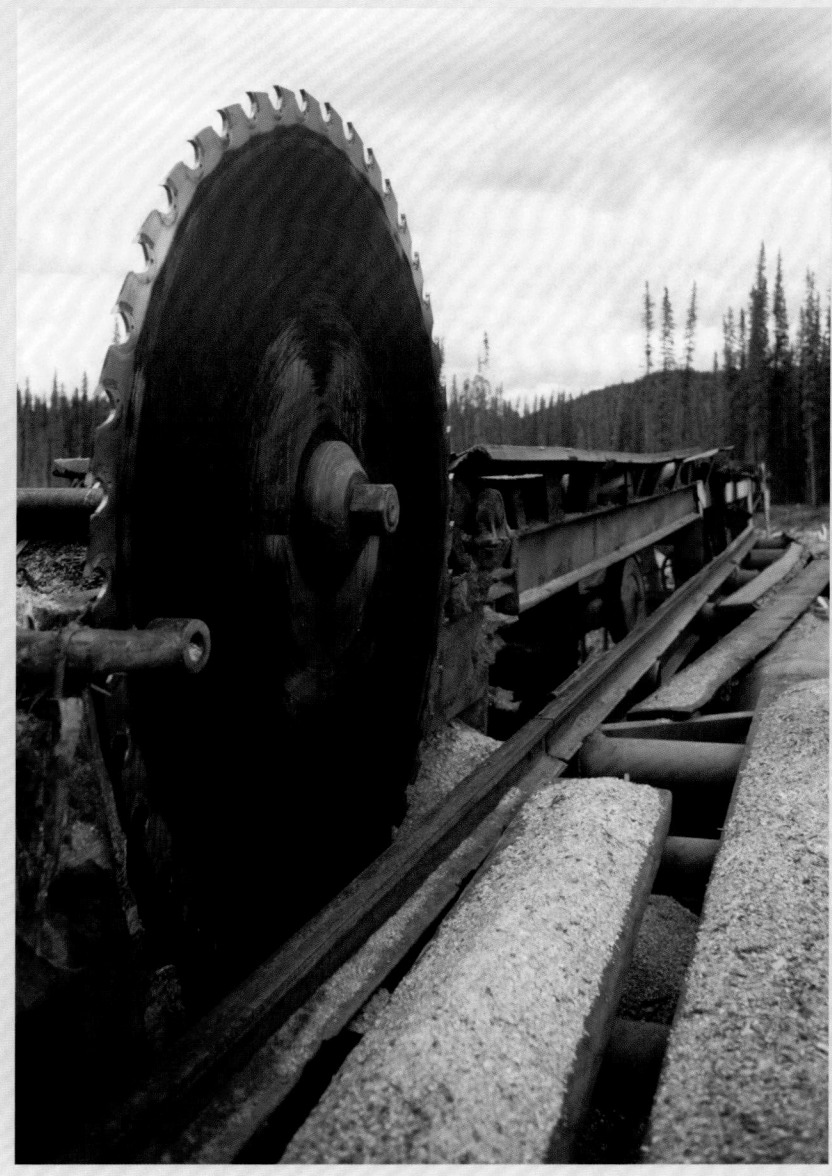

*This mobile sawmill in a small community in northern Canada uses a steel circular saw to cut logs to size.*

*Plain-sawn*    *Quarter-sawn*    *Through-and-through*

*These three different sawing patterns show how shapes of wood are created at the first cut.*

## Sorting and seasoning

Workers called graders check and sort the sawn timber. They grade the wood according to how good it is and look out for **defects**. Different grades of wood are used for various purposes, such as flooring or furniture. At this stage the wood contains a lot of moisture and is called **green wood**. Next it is seasoned, or dried, to prevent it from warping and splitting. The easiest way to do this is by drying the wood in the open air. A quicker method is kiln-drying, when the wood is heated in an oven by warm moving air. This can take hours rather than the weeks it takes to air dry wood.

## Largest sawmill

The world's largest sawmill is the Canadian Canfor Corporation's mill in Houston, British Columbia. It saws about 830,000 cubic metres of softwood a year. The sawmill also produces up to 5000 tonnes of wood pellets from waste, which are used as **biomass fuel** (see page 19).

## USING UP WASTE

Sawmills create a lot of waste sawdust and wood particles. Years ago, workers burned this waste in large ovens to get rid of it. This made a lot of smoke and polluted the air. Today, the waste is used in many different ways. Some is burned to produce energy (see page 19). Some is used to make **fibreboard** (see page 15). Some larger pieces are broken down into wood chips and become a **raw material** for making paper (see page 16). Bark is used in the same way, and some is used to cover or improve soil in gardens.

# Layers and chips

We usually think of wood as a solid block of material. This is wood straight from the tree, which has been cut or sawn into pieces. But most tree trunks are not big enough to produce wide planks or boards.

*Workers sort thin plies (or veneers) in a plywood factory in India.*

## Gluing layers together

We can glue separate boards together, say, to make a tabletop. If this is done well, you can hardly see the joins between the boards. There are many kinds of **engineered wood**, which joins smaller pieces together.

**Plywood** is made from thin sheets of wood, called plies or **veneers**. A machine slices the sheets from a log or thick board as it moves past a fixed knife.

Glued together, the veneers make strong plywood. Manufacturers use an odd number of veneers, three for three-ply wood, five for five-ply, and so on. The **grain** direction of each veneer is at right angles to the next. This adds strength and stops the plywood from warping.

RECYCLE RECYCLE RECYCLE RECYCLE

## REUSING CHIPS

Small pieces of wood from sawmills are made into chipboard. This is a good form of recycling. Some chipboard has a veneer glued to its surface – this is called lamination.

**Blockboard** is made from pieces of wood layered like a sandwich. The two outer layers are thin sheets of wood, like plywood. The filling between the two layers is made of solid blocks of wood. The sandwich is glued together under high pressure.

## Pressing fibres into sheets

To make fibreboard, a machine presses wood fibres, such as sawdust or tiny wood chips, tightly together and then mixes them

## WOOD GRAIN

Have you noticed that most pieces of wood have a streaky pattern? This is called the grain, and it flows in one direction. It comes from the way in which wood fibres join together to form lines. The grain often makes a piece of wood look attractive, and every grain pattern is unique. The grain is important in engineered woods and you can sometimes see where pieces of wood have been stuck together because of the different grain patterns.

with chemicals and **resins**. Fibreboard sheets are used to make walls or cupboards. Some fibreboard has a veneer of wood glued on to the surface to make it look like real wood.

*Long edge pieces of ply are cut and sorted in a Brazilian factory.*

# Made from wood

**Cellulose fibres from wood can make a variety of materials. The most common and important is paper, and today one in ten of the world's trees is grown for paper. Manufacturers also produce a man-made fibre from cellulose which is used for weaving textiles and clothes.**

Wood contains resins and oils which go into inks, perfumes, soaps and many other products. Various trees produce their own special products. Pine trees can produce **turpentine**, and several kinds of tropical trees produce a sappy substance called latex, from which we make rubber.

## Making paper

Most paper is made from softwood trees grown specially for the purpose. At a pulp mill, a machine grinds down softwood logs into wood chips. A chemical dissolves the chips to form a soupy pulp, which then goes to a paper mill. There, the pulp is turned into paper on long machines with many rollers. The papermaking machine mixes pulp and water and spreads it out on a wire mesh, then drains, heats and dries it. This produces large rolls of paper.

*A worker checks a large roll of paper at the end of the papermaking process.*

## Artificial silk

During the 1880s scientists used cellulose from wood to create the first man-made fibre. They heated a mixture of natural fibres with chemicals. Then they forced

*This photo from the 1940s shows a worker checking spools of rayon in a factory in North Carolina, USA.*

the hot, runny resin through tiny holes in a device called a spinneret. This made flexible strands that could be wound on to spools. The inventors called the new substance artificial silk, because they hoped it would replace the expensive silk used to make women's clothing. It was also called viscose, and in 1924 the name was changed to rayon. The fabric became very popular and is still produced today for clothes and furnishings.

## Oil from trees

Artists use an oil called turpentine to thin paints. Turpentine also removes stains from fabric and is an ingredient in some **disinfectants**, **insecticides** and medicines. Its name comes from terebinth, a small Mediterranean tree. Today, the oil comes mainly from pine trees, and from wood as

it is turned into papermaking pulp. The pulp is heated to give off a **vapour**, which cools to produce turpentine.

RECYCLE RECYCLE RECYCLE RECYCLE

### RECYCLED PAPER

Paper is one of the easiest materials to recycle. People put old newspapers and other paper into paper banks. The used paper is cleaned, and chemicals remove the ink. Then it can be turned back into pulp, ready to be used or mixed with fresh wood pulp and turned into recycled paper.

# Burning wood for energy

*These African children have collected firewood for their families.*

**Scientists call all plant and animal matter biomass. Wood forms an important part of the world's biomass. We know that people have burned wood for hundreds of thousands of years for heating and cooking.**

More recently we have learned how to use wood and other plant matter as an energy source to power machines and produce electricity. This is called biomass power.

## Fuel for fires

More than half the wood used in the world every year is burned as fuel. In many African and Asian countries, fuelwood is people's main source of energy. Together, the two continents produce nearly three quarters of the world's wood fuel.

In some **developing countries**, people walk many kilometres every day to collect wood. India is the world's top producer of wood fuel, and more than three quarters of the wood is used for cooking. Only a small part of the wood comes from managed forests, which adds to the problem of deforestation.

*A harvesting machine gathers young willow trees at a plantation in England.*

## Top fuelwood growers

| Country | Million cubic metres |
| --- | --- |
| India | 307 |
| China | 200 |
| Brazil | 140 |
| Ethiopia | 97 |
| Congo (Dem Rep) | 73 |

## Crops for energy

Trees such as poplar and willow grow very quickly. They can be cut down nearly to ground level then will grow again, so farmers can harvest wood regularly. The farmers cut down poplar and willow **plantations** every two years. Every hectare produces up to 90 tonnes of wood to be used as biomass fuel or ground into chips for paper or chipboard.

## Making electricity

Wood chips, sawdust and tree bark can all fuel electric power stations. The wood burns in a **furnace**, which boils water to produce steam. This turns the blades of a **turbine**, which drives a **generator** that produces electricity. In some parts of the world, power plants once powered by coal or oil have changed to burning biomass. In Australia some burn eucalyptus wood.

### FROM SOLID TO GAS OR LIQUID

Solid wood can be turned into a gas by a process called gasification. First a machine called a reactor heats the wood to a very high temperature without much oxygen. It gives off a mixture of gases, including hydrogen and methane, which can drive an electric generator. Another way to convert wood is to use chemicals which break down wood such as poplar to produce a liquid called ethanol. This can be used as a biofuel to replace petrol and drive cars and lorries.

# Working with wood

**Woodworking is one of our oldest crafts. Ancient Egyptian craftsmen made elegant wooden tables, chairs, beds and chests, as well as their famous coffins (see page 22). About 2500 years ago, the ancient Chinese also took up woodworking. Today, this is still an important industry around the world.**

Woodworkers carve, saw, trim and join wood to build houses, boats, furniture and many other items. Carpenters make and repair small wooden objects and larger structures. Joiners make the wooden parts of a building, such as stairs, doors and window frames. Cabinetmakers make high-quality furniture. Many people also enjoy woodworking as a hobby.

## Timber houses

Wooden houses are traditional in many parts of the world, especially near the vast forests of the northern regions. The log cabins built in Canada and Scandinavia are typical. In other places, wood is used in houses which are also made of brick, stone or concrete. Some have a wooden framework. Floors may be made from wooden boards or covered with wooden blocks or tiles, called parquet flooring.

*Many kinds of houses are built on a wooden framework.*

## Woodworking tools

Do-it-yourself woodworkers and professional carpenters use special tools. Woodworkers traditionally use hand tools, but today many are power-driven. A woodworker needs different kinds of saws, such as a strong tenon saw for precise work and a more delicate coping saw for cutting curves and other shapes. A chisel has a sharp cutting edge for shaving wood. Drills and augers bore holes. Various planes and files smooth the surface of wood.

## Joining pieces of wood

Woodworkers use joints to fit pieces of wood together. They may also use glue. These joints can make wooden furniture look more attractive. In a dovetail joint a series of angled tenons fit together. A lap joint is made by overlapping pieces of wood.

In a **mortise** and **tenon** joint the mortise is a hole or slot into which a tenon (or projecting piece) fits.

*Dovetail joints are often used in boxes and frames. Lap joints are usually glued, nailed or screwed. The mortise and tenon joint is used for door frames.*

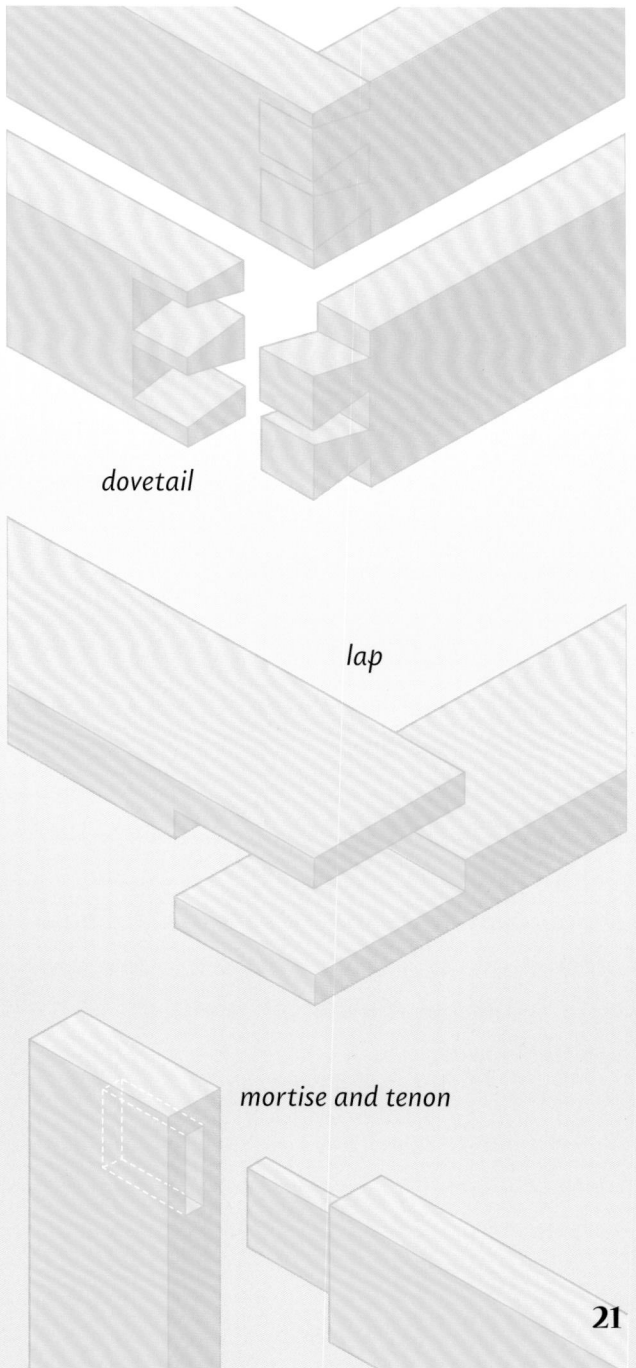

*dovetail*

*lap*

*mortise and tenon*

21

# Making pictures and designs

Artists have carved wood since they began using stone and metal tools thousands of years ago. They later painted on wood, and then learned to put small layers of wood together to make designs. Artists use the different colours and grains of wood, as well as knots and individual patterns. They also carve pictures in wood to use as prints.

## Carving and sculpture

Prehistoric people carved wooden figurines, and made wooden masks to wear at ceremonies. This tradition continues among many African tribes, and their wood-carving influenced great European artists such as Pablo Picasso (1881-1973). Among tribes of the northern forests, Native American craftworkers carved intricate wooden totem poles as well as masks.

## Decorating wood

Native Americans painted their totem poles with bright colours. Wood painting was also a tradition among ancient Egyptians. About 3000 years ago they began decorating the wooden coffins they carved in a human shape, painting scenes on the wood. These often showed dead people being judged before their journey to the underworld in a wooden boat.

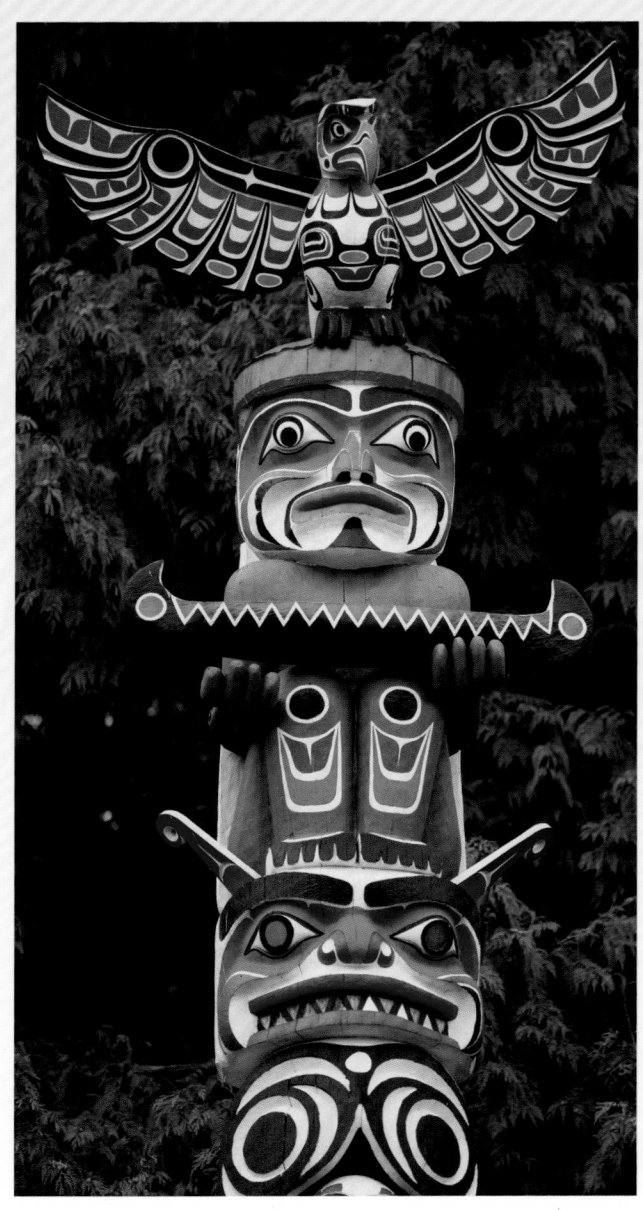

*Native American people of the Northwest Pacific Coast traditionally make totem poles like this one. They usually carve them from cedar wood.*

## Patterns of veneer

Craftworkers in sixteenth-century Flanders (modern Belgium) invented a new way of using wood to make beautiful designs and pictures. They took thin layers of different kinds of wood, called veneers, and fitted shapes together like a jigsaw puzzle to make a picture. This is called marquetry. It became popular in neighbouring France, where cabinetmakers began using the technique to decorate their furniture. They used different coloured woods, ranging from white boxwood though to black ebony.

## Woodcuts

Wood can also be used to print pictures. The process and the picture are both called

*Surrounded by veneers, designer Anita Lear Sancha shows a table top she made by marquetry.*

woodcuts. The ancient Chinese were probably the first to do this. An artist takes a block of wood and cuts away the parts he does not want to appear in the finished print. This leaves a raised picture on the wood. The artist then rolls ink on to the design, and presses the block on to paper. The design is printed in ink on the paper. One of the greatest woodcutters was the German artist Albrecht Dürer (1471-1528). He was followed by many Japanese woodcut artists in the seventeenth century, and their work is still famous today.

# The world's forests today

Forests cover nearly a third of the world's land. So there is more than half a hectare (or 5000 square metres) of forest for every person on Earth. However, in the first decade of this century, forests have shrunk by two per cent every year. That might not sound much, but it means that less and less wood is available as each year passes.

*There are forests on all the world's continents, except for Antarctica in the extreme south.*

## Useful forests

Some forests provide much more useful wood than others. The United Nations' Food and Agriculture Organization (FAO) says that just over a third of the world's forests are 'productive'. The top five countries with productive forest plantations are China, the USA, Russia, Brazil and Sudan.

## Trees in danger

Just as there are many endangered species of animals in the world, many kinds of trees are also in danger of dying out. They include many tropical trees from the rainforests of South America, Africa and Asia such as the King William and Parana pine, mahogany, satinwood, teak and walnut.

## RENEWABLE RESOURCE

Trees are a renewable resource so long as forests are properly managed. That means planting new trees all the time and not cutting down too many trees at one time. The international Forest Stewardship Council (FSC) puts its logo on products (including paper) that are made from trees in well-managed forests. The FSC controls more than 109 million hectares of forest around the world, but this is less than a tenth of the total.

## Where do trees grow?

The only areas where trees don't grow are:
• in the polar regions, where it is too cold;
• in deserts, where it is too dry; and
• in areas where a lot of people live, who cut down the trees and do not plant new ones.

Much of the world's softwood (see page 11) grows in enormous forests that stretch across the north of Asia, North America and Europe. Many hardwoods grow in the mild regions of the world, above and below the **tropics**. **Tropical rainforests** have the most varied trees, and most are broad-leaved evergreens. Deforestation is a particular problem in rainforests. Environmental organizations are trying to protect our rainforests and stop the clearing of trees.

*Ovens turn wood into charcoal in this area of cleared rainforest in northern Brazil.*

25

# Recycling wood

Wood can be recycled in many different ways. Timbers from old buildings can be reused in new ones. Unusable old wood is ground down into wood chips to make biomass fuel, or to make chipboard or pulp for paper. Recently, environmental groups such as Greenpeace and Friends of the Earth have tried to persuade everyone to use more recycled materials, including wood.

## New life for old timber

When an old building is demolished or renovated, workers can carefully take out the timber. They sell it to timber merchants, who treat the wood then sell it on. First, they scan the wood with a metal detector and remove all nails, screws or other metal bits. Then they saw it down to a new size, cutting away any pieces or edges that are damaged or rotten. The recycled timber can make new floors, beams or outside decking.

## Choosing and using wood

Friends of the Earth suggest that this is the way we should all choose wood.
• Repair, restore or adapt something you already have that is made of wood. This costs less than buying or making something new and is far better for the world's forests.

*A wood-chip mountain in southern Chile. The chips are loaded on to barges and lorries to go to factories.*

*These workers use traditional methods to strip cork in Sardinia, Italy.*

• Buy second-hand, recycled, reclaimed or waste timber. This is a better choice than buying new wood.
• Buy locally produced timber products approved by the Forest Stewardship Council (FSC) (see page 25).

## New paper for old

Paper (made from wood) is one of the easiest materials to recycle. About 43 per cent of the world's paper is recycled and this figure is increasing. You can take waste newspapers, magazines and other paper to a nearby paper bank. Many local authorities also collect paper for recycling.

Recycled waste paper often includes several different types made from various fibres, for example, office waste paper, newsprint, card and board. These are usually sorted before being turned back into pulp. The pulp can then be used to make paper of the same or

### RECYCLED AT SOURCE

One wood product renews itself on the tree. This is cork, which comes from trees called cork oaks. They grow in Portugal, Spain and Italy. Their thick, light outer bark makes the natural cork that we use as bottle stoppers, especially for wine. Cork is also used for floors, mats and other items. Cork-strippers cut the bark from a tree every nine years. This does not harm the tree and the bark regrows until it is ready to be harvested again nine years later. Many wine bottles today have plastic or metal stoppers, which has harmed the cork industry. Cork-oak farmers are struggling to survive.

lower quality than the original paper. It cannot be used to make higher quality paper unless it is mixed with new pulp.

RECYCLE RECYCLE RECYCLE

# Wood in the future

We will need more and more wood in the future, for building houses and making furniture and paper. Wood is likely to become even more important to us as a source of renewable energy. Most people like the look and feel of wood, but perhaps we have more to learn about the ways in which we can use wood.

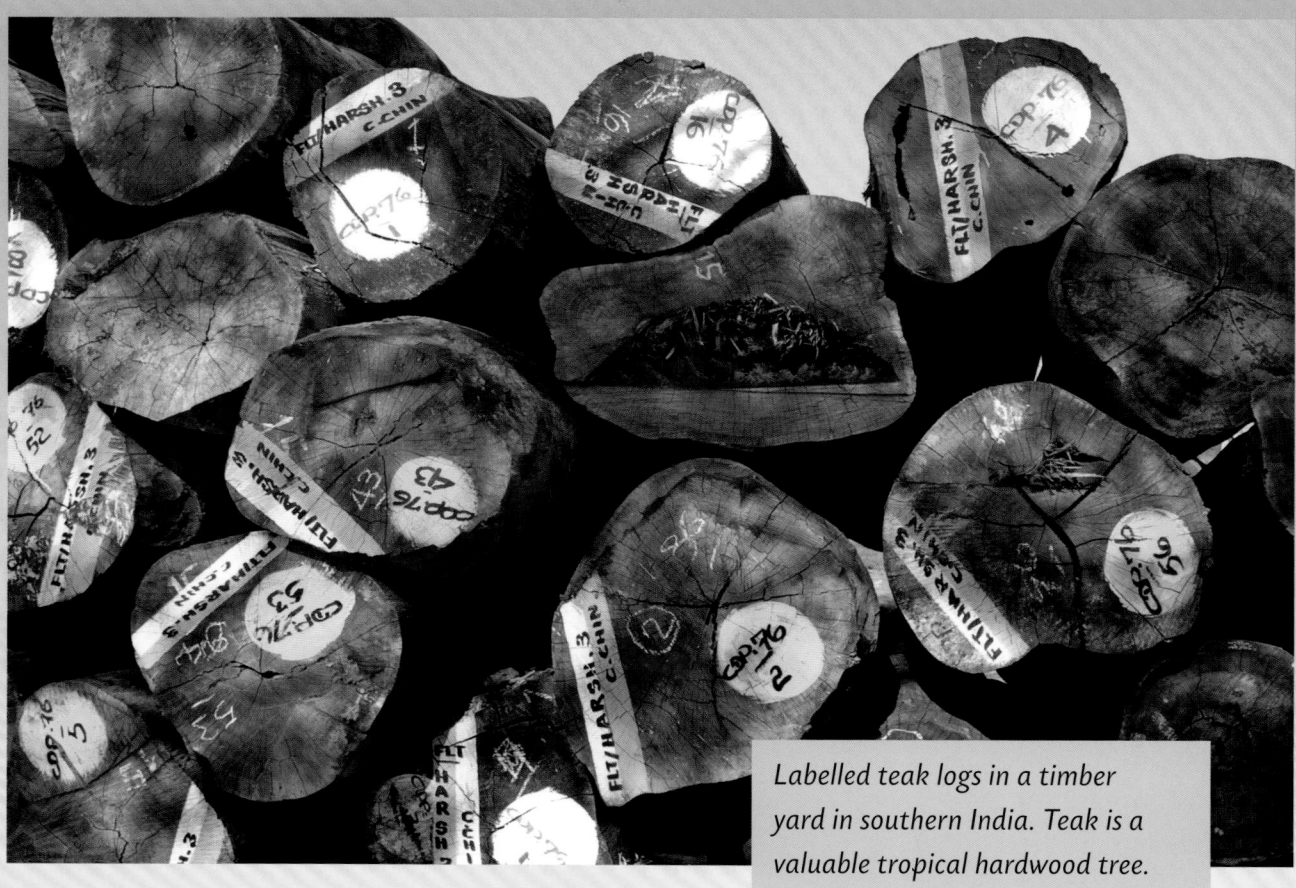

*Labelled teak logs in a timber yard in southern India. Teak is a valuable tropical hardwood tree.*

## Learning from wood

There may be a lot more that botanists and other scientists can learn about wood. At the Royal Institute of Technology in Stockholm, Sweden, researchers are working on a project called Biomime. They are studying wood fibres and cell walls, to see whether we can imitate nature and make new wood-like materials. These could be similar to rayon (see page 17), and might lead on to new artificial fibres.

*These threadlike cellulose fibres have been magnified 140 times by a microscope. Nanotechnology might make it possible to combine the fibres with other materials.*

## Changing the nature of wood

An alternative to imitating wood is to try to change it. Scientists already know how to alter plants and animals by modifying, or changing, their genes. They all have biological sets of instructions within their cells. These coded instructions are carried by genes, which pass on the code to the next generation. So scientists could change the qualities of wood. They could make some wood harder or more grainy, for example. This process is called **genetic modification (GM)**. Many environmentalists say that GM crops are unnatural and could be dangerous to the environment and human health.

## Wood on a tiny scale

More future changes might come from **nanotechnology**, which uses materials in tiny sizes. Researchers in Canada are using this technology to take tiny particles of cellulose in wood and combine them with other materials. The particles are just 20 nanometres (billionths of a metre) long. Scientists want to combine them with particles of other materials, such as plastics or metals, to make new substances. These could be strong but light, and useful in aircraft, spacecraft and other vehicles.

## Future forests

More and more forests will be specially planted and managed in future. People in the forestry industry will want to plant forests of a small number of tree species, because these are easier to grow and control. They will grow trees especially for building, furniture or paper pulp. Environmentalists want to protect the world's wide range of trees. Many once grew in mixed forests, which are not so useful for wood as a material.

# Glossary

**biomass fuel**   A substance produced from plant or animal matter that provides power; also called biofuel.

**blockboard**   A block of wood with thin sheets of wood glued on.

**carbon dioxide** ($CO_2$)   A greenhouse gas given off when fossil fuels (such as coal, oil or gas) are burned.

**cedar**   An evergreen cone-bearing tree.

**cellulose**   A substance that makes up the cell walls of plants.

**charcoal**   A black form of carbon made by heating wood.

**deciduous**   Describes a tree that sheds its leaves in autumn.

**defect**   A fault or blemish.

**deforestation**   Cutting down trees and removing woods and forests.

**developing countries**   Poorer parts of the world where industry and technology are not advanced.

**disinfectant**   A substance that destroys tiny organisms that cause disease.

**engineered wood**   Wood pieces joined together, for example plywood.

**evergreen**   Describes a tree that keeps its leaves all year round.

**fibreboard**   A wooden material made by pressing wood fibres into sheets.

**flammable**   Describes something that can easily catch fire.

**flint**   A hard grey-black rock.

**furnace**   An oven-like container for heating materials to very high temperatures.

**galley**   A large ship with oars and sails.

**generator**   A machine that turns mechanical energy into electrical energy.

**genetic modification**   Using technology to change the genes of plants or animals and alter their characteristics.

**grain**   Wood grain is the pattern made by the way fibres join together to make lines.

**green wood**   Newly cut wood.

**hardboard**   Wooden sheets made by pressing wood chips and sawdust together.

**hardwood**   Wood from a broad-leaved, deciduous tree, such as an oak.

**heartwood**   The dark, older wood at the centre of a tree trunk.

**hydrant**   A water pipe in the street that firefighters can use.

**insecticide**   A chemical that kills insects.

**lignin**   A substance that holds plant fibres together and makes plants rigid and woody.

**mortise**   A hole or slot cut into wood; a tenon fits into it to make a joint.

**nanotechnology**   Technology that uses materials in tiny, microscopic sizes.

**photosynthesis**   The process plants use to make their own food from carbon dioxide and water.

**plantation**   A large group of trees planted in one area.

**plough**   A heavy farming tool that breaks up soil.

**plywood**   Wooden board made by pressing and gluing together thin layers of wood.

**pollution**   Damage to the environment caused by harmful substances.

**prehistoric**   Describes the time before people recorded history in writing.

**raw material**   A natural material, such as wood, before it is processed and used to make something.

**resin**   A sticky substance produced by some plants.

**sapwood**   The light, softer wood between a tree's bark and heartwood.

**softwood**   Wood from a needle-leaved, evergreen tree, such as a pine.

**tenon**   A projecting piece of wood that fits into a mortise to form a joint.

**tropical rainforest**   Thick evergreen forest in tropical areas with heavy rainfall.

**tropics**   The world's warmest regions just above and below the equator (the imaginary line around the middle of the Earth).

**turbine**   A machine with rotating blades that turn a shaft.

**turf**   Soil with grass growing on it.

**turpentine**   An oil that comes mainly from pine trees.

**vapour**   A moist gas.

**veneer**   A thin layer of wood fixed to another material.

**xylem**   A scientific word for plant tissue or wood.

# Websites

Information on the Forest Stewardship Council (see page 25) and its work managing the world's forests, including facts and figures.
www.fsc.org

A description of the processes involved in making wood and plywood, concentrating on saving energy.
www.fao.org/docrep/t0269e/t0269e03.htm

All about reusing and recycling wood by the Wood Recyclers' Association.
www.woodrecyclers.org/recycling.php

News on Tree for All – a project that gives children the chance to plant trees.
www.treeforall.org.uk

Fascinating facts about cork and how it is produced.
www.corkfacts.com/natlcrk11.htm

# Index